Spring
meditations

JOHN BARTUNEK, LC, STD

D1472376

Imprimi Potest:
Stephen T. Rehrauer, CSsR, Provincial
Denver Province, the Redemptorists

Imprimi Potest:
Fr. John Connor, LC, Territorial Director
Territory of Northern America, Legionaries of Christ

Published by Liguori Publications
Liguori, Missouri 63057

To order, visit Liguori.org or call 800-325-9521.

Library of Congress Cataloging-in-Publication Data

Names: Bartunek, John, author.
Title: Spring meditations / John Bartunek, LC, STD
Description: First Edition. | Liguori : Liguori Publications, 2016.
Identifiers: LCCN 2015043045 (print) | LCCN 2015045673 (ebook)
    ISBN 9780764825613 | ISBN 9780764870125 ()
Subjects: LCSH: Spring—Religious aspects—Christianity—Meditations.
    Spiritual exercises.
Classification: LCC BV135.S67 B37 2016 (print) | LCC BV135.S67 (ebook) |' DDC
    242—dc23
LC record available at http://lccn.loc.gov/2015043045

Liguori Publications, a nonprofit corporation, is an apostolate of the Redemptorists. To learn more about the Redemptorists, visit Redemptorists.com.

Printed in the United States of America

20 19 18 17 16 / 5 4 3 2 1

First Edition

Table of Contents

Introduction

We don't need scientific studies to tell us that today's culture is out of touch with nature, even though plenty of such studies exist. Not only does our world have various social pockets engaged in industrial activities that have alarming effects on the environment, but also few of us post-modern people are able to live our lives in harmony with the natural rhythms of the earth.

In fact, we tend to ignore them, whether consciously or not. We can make day seem like night and night seem like day. We can make winter feel like summer and summer feel like winter. We can travel from the tropics to the tundra in less than a day, from the mountains to the sea in an afternoon. We can find whatever fruit or vegetable we want in our local grocery store, regardless of the season.

In short, our natural environment has become a kind of add-on to our lives. We feel the pangs of weather changes and the panic of natural disasters, but our day-to-day lives, our month-to-month lives, our year-to-year lives have, in general, gotten out of synch with the natural rhythms of the earth we were created to inhabit.

This causes problems. As humans, we are *meant* to unfold our lives in harmony with the natural world. The seasons, the processes of nature, the *rhythms* of this world—our world—were created out of love and given to us as a home. They have something to tell us about our deeper identity, the purpose of our life, the way to fully live life. By cutting us off from direct, regular, and necessary contact with this natural environment, our technology-laden culture is threatening to sever an ancient and irreplaceable link to authentic wisdom.

A Needed Return to Natural Wisdom

The bite-size meditations in this first of four books dedicated to the natural seasons will provide you with some space to remember and reconnect with this essential dimension of your humanity. That, by the way, is what we mean by "meditation": giving yourself the time and space, both physically and psychologically, to reflect calmly but deeply on important spiritual values. It is our sincere hope that by doing so you will experience a spiritual and emotional revitalization. You will be able to escape from the ceaseless, inhuman, digitized grind of life and regain some balance.

Not that you aren't spiritual now, but even though you have hope, courage, faith, and love, you still feel a hunger to have *more:* A deeper faith, a more vibrant hope, a more dynamic courage. That's one of the great things about spiritual values—they can always keep growing.

Avoiding the Rush

This volume only contains twelve meditations, one per week of the season. But at the end of each meditation you will find some suggested activities to help you absorb the nourishing truths the meditation explained (the *Making It Your Own* sections). A good way to make use of this book is to read a meditation at the beginning of the week underlining, highlighting, and writing in the margins as you reflect on what you read. Then for the rest of the week, take time each day to review your highlights and to put into practice one of the suggested activities. Following that method will assure that whatever good ideas you find as you read will have sufficient time and space to seep from your mind into your heart and your spirit, fostering personal renewal.

Getting Personal

These meditations contain many personal anecdotes that I think help illustrate my points. I also hope that making myself vulnerable in this way will encourage you to reflect on the richness of your own life experience to find the lessons, the nuggets of wisdom, that God, in his generous providence, always offers to you.

May this small volume of simple meditations on the season of spring be a window through which you can discover, once again, the "dearest freshness deep down things"[1] that have always nourished what is best in the human spirit.

---

[1] From Gerard Manley Hopkins' poem "God's Grandeur"

Chapter 1: *Hope*

Winter was harsh. Cold and deadening, stormy and aggressive, it tried, so it seemed, to do away with any possibility of spring. It does that every year. Every winter grips the earth with a freezing grasp until nature is little more than a brittle skeleton coated with ice and dripping with icicles and frozen beyond breath.

And yet, spring always comes. Winter never wins the final battle. The cold, seemingly lifeless limbs outlast the ice. The warmer sun melts the freezing grip and calls forth the hidden breath while new life begins to stir.

New life. An old saying reminds us that where there is life, there is hope. But isn't it also true that where there is hope, there is life? Hope feeds on the past and nourishes the future. In the midst of even the longest winter, we can look forward to spring because the past has taught us that spring always comes. Life is more powerful than death because life is a gift from God who is love, and love is eternal.

A hopeful person is a hope-filled person. This is one of the lessons spring teaches us. After the death of winter comes the resurrection of spring. Nature revels in resurrection, and it encourages us to hope. Just like winter giving way to spring's irrepressible vitality, our moral and emotional winters fade and are transformed by the risen Lord.

When I was working in Chicago before joining the seminary I used to travel by train. You can get pretty much anywhere in that city using the train system, if you're willing. I used to like the longer train rides in the off hours, when there was enough room to actually take a seat. I preferred the window seats. I would gaze at the city passing by while I made my way to wherever I needed to go. I coveted time to think, reflect, and pray during those days because I could hear God's call reverberating in my heart. But life was so noisy that I would often lose track of that call. Long train rides with a window seat would help the noise fall away and give me a chance to listen to God's voice whispering in my soul.

I would see many beautiful things on those rides: the amazing architecture of the city, the gorgeous shore and horizon of Lake Michigan, the bustle of a young population eager to work hard and get ahead.

One image from those trips has stuck with me more than any other, but it's not what most people would call beautiful, at least not at first glance.

The train was speeding through a poverty-stricken, dilapidated section of the city, with boarded-up stores, burnt-out buildings, and collapsing houses pockmarking the landscape. I felt the melancholy. I felt the weight of the sadness. It was heavy, very heavy. I wasn't catching even a whiff of hope.

Then the train slowed and came to a stop, and I found myself looking at an empty parking lot surrounded by a precariously leaning fence. The asphalt was cracked, and broken pieces of the asphalt were piled up like rubble after a bombing. Because the train had stopped I had a chance for more than a quick glance. As I continued to gaze at the empty lot, I saw more than just rubble and failure. In the cracks of the asphalt, lush green grass and brightly colored wildflowers were bursting up toward the sky. Ivy and flowers with many colors were climbing joyfully along the leaning fence. A flowering shrub rejoiced in the corner, blissfully unaware of its dire need for pruning.

Here was new life. Here were living creatures that hadn't been told that this neighborhood was dead and hopeless. Amidst the angry, broken blacktop and the rusty links of the hapless fence a cheery grin winked out at me. Life wins. Hope fails not. Love is the deepest core of all things and will always find a way to sing out anew from the darkest, coldest winter, to grow and blossom in the cracks of the pavement.

One of my favorite saint stories comes from third-century Rome, where deacon St. Lawrence was the pope's right-hand man, in charge of the local church's finances and of taking care of the poor.

It was one of those periods in history when Christians were being persecuted for refusing to worship the false gods of a tyrannical state. Rome's governor arrested the pope and some other churchmen, condemning them to execution for treason against the Roman deities. He had heard that St. Lawrence was in charge of the treasury, so when questioning the deacon he asked about the riches of the church. Lawrence agreed to hand those riches over but asked for a few days to gather them together.

During that time, he sold the church's assets and gave them to the city's poor. When he returned to the governor he brought along homeless and ill beggars. He announced to the governor, "Behold the treasures of the Church." The governor was furious and sentenced Lawrence to be grilled to death over a bed of hot coals.

While Lawrence was in prison the night before his execution, he was full of energy, of joy. He stayed awake praying and sang hymns of praise to the Lord. His guard couldn't understand it. Finally he approached the prisoner and asked him why he was so overjoyed when his execution was merely hours away. Saint Lawrence looked him in the eye and smiled, telling him what he was looking forward to: eternal life with God in heaven, seeing the Creator face to face, an everlasting embrace of love with the origin of all that was good in the world. Thus began a long conversation about the Gospel, at the end of which the guard asked to be baptized. He also became a saint, and a martyr, just like Lawrence. He is known as St. Romanus.

Lawrence was a human spring, filled with hope. This hope gave him strength to resist the most powerful worldly authorities. It gave him purpose and sharpened his wits. It overflowed into energy and enthusiasm even when it required him to give up all the possibilities of life on earth in order to be faithful to his friendship with God. It made him a light in the darkness, a tender but riveting blossom sprouting from the cold and wintry stones of a prison cell.

Do you want to be a hopeful person? I do. Certain days I feel the vitality of hope coursing through my veins. Other days it seems my veins are still and lifeless, discouragement and frustration grip my heart with a freezing grasp. But when that happens, I know what to do. Our souls aren't merely natural; they are spiritual. We don't have to wait for spring to feel the warmth of hope. We have the capacity to remember the springs that have passed and to contemplate the sureness of the springs to come. That thought can bring spring to our minds and hearts whenever we need it. Even when we find ourselves in a prison, condemned, rejected, humiliated, with nothing left for us on earth—even then—we can hope.

Making It Your Own

† Choose one sentence from this chapter that really resonated in your heart or compose a one-sentence summary. Write it on a sticky note. Put it where you will see it throughout the week. Let it become a reminder of the truth that winter never wins.

† Many people criticize religious faith because they don't understand why there is so much evil and suffering in the world. But the deeper mystery, the harder question, is to fathom why there is so much good and beauty in the world. Take five minutes each day this week to write down the good things that have come to you in life. Describe them in detail. Think about them. Let the past feed your hope.

† What types of activities feed *your* hope? Maybe going for a bike ride or a walk seems to refresh you. Maybe reading children's stories or good fiction seems to encourage

you. Maybe taking quiet time to pray in a beautiful church or chapel strengthens you. Identify your top three hope-feeding activities and do each of them at least once this week.

† What types of activities tend to drain your hope? Maybe watching the news makes you feel negative and pessimistic. Maybe spending too much time online makes you feel distracted and stressed. Maybe there are some relationships in your life that bring you down instead of building you up. What can you do about these hope-drainers?

† Jesus rose from the dead during spring. How often do you think about his resurrection? What does it really mean for you? Take time this week to get out your Bible and go to the end of any of the four Gospels to read the narration of Christ's resurrection. Read it slowly and thoughtfully. Underline phrases that resonate in your heart and maybe even memorize one of them. Let God's word touch your soul.

† Who do you know who seems to be a hope-filled person? Take time to visit with that person this week. Ask where the person's hope comes from and what it means for him or her.

† Children are naturally the "spring" of the human family. They are the new life. Find a way to let the wisdom of a child's innocence and hope warm your heart, too: "Amen, I say to you, unless you turn and become like children, you will not enter the kingdom of heaven" (Matthew 18:3).

Chapter 2: *Courage*

The earliest signs of spring are so small: tiny sprouts peeking through patches of muddy grass; fragile buds on brittle branches tentatively expanding; tiny sparrows gathering to build a new nest in a winter-hardened tree. These are the courageous gestures of spring, lessons from nature that inspire us to follow their example.

Courage is one of those curious words. We feel like we know what it means, but when someone asks us to define it we discover that it's not so clear in our minds. *What is courage?* They say to us, and we answer, *Courage is, well, it's, I mean, it's like being courageous, you know?*

Through the ages, philosophers have discerned courage to be one of the four cardinal virtues (the primary virtues that are like hinges upon which all the other virtues swing). Courage has to do with how we behave in the face of obstacles and difficulties. The determined pursuit of a worthy goal even in the face of opposition and hardship, like the sprout that pops up in the first days of spring, that's the essence of courage.

In English we have a revealing counterpart to courage: *discourage* and *discouragement*. When someone gives in to discouragement, he no longer has the energy to move forward. He gives up. The worthy goal remains worthy but out of reach. At times, when we feel the weight of discouragement, we need something to come and boost our spirits to get us back on track; we need to be *encouraged*.

Discouragement never comes from God. If, in his providence, he has planted a desire in our hearts, he hasn't done so to torture us. He will give us the strength, guidance, and assistance we need to overcome every obstacle and fulfill it. His providence tells the tiny seed when to start sprouting, the bud when to start expanding, the sparrow when to start building its nest. When he whispers something in our hearts, that whisper is enough. All we need to do is keep going, being brave in the face of difficulties.

When I felt God's call to the priesthood, I ran into an obstacle from a surprising source: my dad. I was a recent college graduate with lots of career possibilities, as well as a recent convert to Catholicism. I had fallen in love with the Church and felt such a clear and strong call to wed the Church (which is how I understood the priesthood) that I couldn't deny it. Following that call meant leaving behind a lot of other hopes and dreams, like getting married and having a family, pursuing my long-treasured professional ambitions, and continuing to be in control of decisions about where I would live and how I would spend my time. I felt the sting of these sacrifices, but that sting was nothing compared with the deep enthusiasm and excitement I felt toward serving God and his people as a priest.

Then I told my dad. He had no religious faith at that period of his life. He couldn't understand what I was telling him. He couldn't envision how any normal person could ever be happy as a Catholic priest. He made his sentiments crystal clear to me. We had a fiery discussion during which he told me as directly and vehemently as you can imagine that he could think of no bigger waste of a life than to be a celibate priest.

It was hard for me to hear. It was hard for me to argue against his affirmations that I was throwing away so many gifts and opportunities that he had worked so hard to give me. From his perspective, that was the plain truth. Without faith, how could anyone value the priesthood?

He did everything he could to deter me from joining the seminary. It seemed that in choosing to follow God's call I would have to lay on the altar even my precious friendship with my dad. He was that dead-set against my choice.

I really did feel like a little sprout peeking through the muddy soil in early spring, surrounded by forces more powerful than me. And yet, somehow, the conviction that God was asking this of me was stronger than my fears. Somehow God's whisper in the heart of my heart convinced me that Providence would work it out, that it was going to be OK.

And it was. I entered the seminary, was ordained, and eleven years after my ordination I was able to bring God's mercy to accompany my dad on his deathbed.

Courage is a major theme in salvation history. Whenever God chooses someone for a special task, accepting the call requires an act of bravery. That bravery flows from knowing that God is faithful, that he will support us as we strive to give him glory by living life to the full.

When Moses died and Joshua had to take over leadership of God's Chosen People, he was nervous. Joshua was the one who had to lead the Israelites across the Jordon to take possession of the Promised Land. The Bible records how God *encouraged* Joshua to take up what seemed an impossible task. Notice how many times the Lord has to repeat his encouragement, a sure sign Joshua was feeling scared, inadequate, and intimidated:

[T]he LORD said to Moses' aide Joshua…As I was with Moses, I will be with you: I will not leave you nor forsake you. *Be strong and steadfast*, so that you may give this people possession of the land I swore to their ancestors that I would give them. Only *be strong and steadfast*, being careful to observe the entire law which Moses my servant enjoined on you… I command you: *be strong and steadfast!* Do not fear nor be dismayed, for the LORD, your God, is with you wherever you go" (Joshua 1:1, 5–7, 9, emphasis added).

Jesus said something similar to his Twelve Apostles during the Last Supper. As he prepared them for the horrible experience of his Crucifixion and the hard work of building his Church, he explained: "I have told you this so that you might have peace in me. In the world you will have trouble, but take courage, I have conquered the world" (John 16:33).

When we are truly following God's voice in our hearts, we can rest assured that no obstacle will be too big, no difficulty too hard. With the Lord at our side, we can always be courageous.

These days, we need courage for everything. In some areas of the world, even going to Mass or praying to Jesus requires the courage to take your life into your hands. Many of our brothers and sisters in faith have lost their lives for nothing less.

For most of us, however, courage is needed in less dramatic situations. Being faithful at home, being honest at work, being responsible to the duties of our state in life, these fundamental requirements of a truly human life face more and more opposition in our rapidly decaying culture.

The world around us is full of pressures and influences that constantly try to deceive and weaken us. To follow God's plan for human life, to follow the Ten Commandments, and the most basic laws of human nature has now become countercultural. In such an environment, to be true to the ever-ancient and ever-new wisdom of Christ and his Church requires courage, the courage only God can give.

The world will give us trouble, but we can take courage, because the God who whispers in our hearts is the same God who made the soil and gave the seed its original spark of life.

Making It Your Own

† Choose one sentence from this chapter that really resonated in your heart or compose a one-sentence summary. Write it on a sticky note. Put it where you will see it throughout the week so that it *encourages* you to face up to the obstacles thrown at you.

† Take time to think about a situation in your past that required courage. Describe what you felt. Write it down to grow in self-knowledge and self-awareness.

† What tends to discourage you? Why? What can you do about it? Think ahead and identify a situation or encounter that you may have during the coming week where you will feel discouragement. Plan ahead to keep up your courage.

† What courageous decision or behavior is God whispering for you to follow right now? How have you been responding up to this point? How would you like to respond? Write down what it would take for you to say yes to the Lord, then speak to him about it in prayer.

† What fears most commonly arise in your heart and mind? Where are they rooted? How do you usually cope with them? Find someone you trust—a mentor, a spiritual director, someone you know is wise—and set up a time to talk with that individual about your fears.

† What encourages you? Why? Where do you go to find encouragement when you need it? This week, go there at least once, even if you don't feel a strong need for encouragement.

† Who in your circle of influence needs encouragement? What could you do to help give it to them? Write down at least three different possibilities. Choose one of them and commit to doing it this week. Write it in your calendar to help you remember it.

Chapter 3: *Love*

Why do *so many* daisies pop up in spring meadows? Why do *so many* leaves appear when spring arrives? Why does a cherry tree put out *so many* cherry blossoms? What is the meaning of this abundance? It is an image of true love.

True love is not merely a feeling. True love is giving—self-giving. True love is opening up the treasures of our life, as scanty as those treasures may seem, and sharing them with others who are in need. True love is reaching out to the wider world and pouring into it whatever goodness we can find within ourselves, just like a spring blossom opens its petals as wide as it can and pours out its fragrance and its color and its promise of new life. This is true love, forgetting oneself and simply giving. And this is beautiful. It's no coincidence that flowers are a traditional and symbolic gift between lovers. It's no coincidence that flowers are the natural icons of beauty. The flower is the place where a plant opens itself to the world and gives. Love is the place where we do the same.

What happens to the tree when its blossoms spread and pour themselves out? Fruitfulness, growth, expansion, multiplication. Only by giving does the tree become fertile and produce fruit. Just so, we can only grow and produce spiritual fruit in our lives when we open and give of ourselves.

This is counterintuitive, so we have to think about it. Usually when we give something away it means we have less. We are impoverished. If I give away $20, I am poorer by $20. If I give away my car, I have to take the bus. If I give away my lunch, I have to go hungry. But this is the *material* perspective. Our deeper identity is spiritual, which provides a new perspective.

When we love, when we give of ourselves or give what we have for the good of our neighbor, our spirit blooms and flourishes and produces fruit: "the fruit of the Spirit is love, joy, peace, patience, kindness, generosity, faithfulness, gentleness, self-control" (Galatians 5:22–23). This is because we are created in God's image, and "God is love" (1 John 4:8).

When we love truly, we fulfill what we were created for, and that makes us flourish. The more we give of ourselves for the good of others, the more we receive in return from that gift, just as a tree that puts out more blossoms bears more fruit.

One summer after college I received a fellowship to spend several months working and studying in a museum in Venice, Italy. The sponsor made all the living arrangements for the fellowship recipients, and I was assigned a room in a lovely old palazzo just off the Grand Canal. My host was a longtime patron of the museum, a woman of extraordinary spiritual beauty, a Serbian countess and widow who happened to be 105 years old.

The summer that I boarded with her was a spiritually trying season of my life. I had been a nondenominational Christian for years but had begun to seriously explore the Catholic Church. Many factors from my past made me suspicious of the Catholic faith, but many more were leading me inexorably into it. I was in crisis, and part of me wanted to run away. I was rootless, anguished, and very vulnerable to temptations of all kinds.

When I arrived in Venice, I was impressed by the countess' noble family background and her clearly gracious and civilized way of being. I was also impressed that she was so sharp and self-sufficient at her advanced age. But I was less interested in spending time with her than with the other fellowship recipients and our growing circle of Venetian friends.

That changed as the summer progressed. Somehow, like a magnet, the countess' inner beauty began to draw me toward her. I began to prefer spending my evenings at home, watching the sun go down through the palazzo's living-room windows and having a drink with the countess, preparing dinner with her, chatting, and, well, just *being* with her.

She was different. She didn't look like a cherry tree in full flower (after 105 years, who would?). But that's what her spirit was like. Being in her presence was like picnicking in a park full of blossoming fruit trees. Her heart was a spiritual garden in perpetual bloom, pouring forth the sweet aroma of wisdom, goodness, and generosity so abundantly that I didn't want to go anywhere else.

We became friends that summer, but it was a brief friendship. She passed away a few months later. But what she gave me, what she taught me, stayed. She was my spiritual lifeline during that delicate and dangerous season of my life. Her love, her inner springtime, somehow enabled me to overcome my fears and give to God what he was asking of me. It enabled me to take a tentative step down the path of spiritual generosity when I was afraid. When I was dead-set on clinging to myself instead of opening up and pouring myself out, the spiritual love of the countess helped me blossom.

Jesus talked about this kind of love a lot. He didn't complicate it. He just lived it. He lived it by sacrificing his own life on the cross to atone for the sins of our fallen human race. That was Good Friday. He gave his life to rebuild communion between God and the rebellious human family. And what was the result? He rose from the dead three days later, on Easter. The life he gave was mortal; the life he rose to is eternal. That's how Jesus lived the love he preached.

But he preached it, too, powerfully and beautifully, over and over again. He put it in terms that working-class people could understand by referring to shares of grain being distributed:

> Give, and gifts will be yours; good measure, pressed down and shaken up and running over, will be poured into your lap; the measure you award to others is the measure that will be awarded to you (Luke 6:38, *Knox Bible*).

He encouraged all of us not to be afraid of true love, self-forgetful love, the love that gives of itself even when it seems we have nothing left to give:

> "Amen, amen, I say to you, unless a grain of wheat falls to the ground and dies, it remains just a grain of wheat; but if it dies, it produces much fruit. Whoever loves his life loses it, and whoever hates his life in this world will preserve it for eternal life" (John 12:24–25).

He explained it simply: "There is more happiness in giving than receiving" (Acts 20:35, *Jerusalem Bible*).

Imagine springtime without blossoms and flowers. A springtime that was afraid to open itself up and pour itself out into the wider world, a springtime that refused to give of its own life out of fear or greed. That would be the last of springtime, the end of the ever-growing and flowing cycle of new, fruitful, beautiful life. A person who doesn't learn to love never makes it into spring.

Look at the spring blossoms, the flowers, the abundant outpouring of life that is an ode to love, a visual symphony showcasing the path to true happiness. Without self-giving, without generosity, without pouring the good gifts we have received (however small and poor they may seem) into the world so they can be shared by others, the moral winter of fear and self-absorption will never be overcome.

It's hard for us to love truly. Instinctively, we prefer to *get* rather than *give*. The default setting for our wounded human nature is more like a black hole than a healthy sun. And yet our spirit will never flourish unless we learn this lesson, and we *can* learn it. Look at the blossoms; listen to their message. Will you let them be your teacher?

Making It Your Own

† Choose one sentence from this chapter that really resonated in your heart or compose a one-sentence summary. Write it on a sticky note. Put it where you'll see it throughout the week as a reminder for you to smell the sweet aroma of love and give a good measure of your self to those around you.

† Think about the people in your life who have modeled true love for you. Savor the love you have received from them and thank God for them. This week, reach out to one and thank him or her, expressing what he or she has meant to you.

† Take time this week to sit and reflect on the key relationships in your life. Ask yourself what you expect from those relationships. Then ask what you are pouring into them. How could you apply Jesus' saying, "There is more happiness in giving than in receiving" to each of those relationships. Make a concrete resolution about how you will give of yourself in a special way this week in one of those relationships.

† Take time this week to write all the ways you consume entertainment. Reflect on the effect that each of those activities (TV shows, video games, movies, happy hours, etc.) has on your soul. How would you describe that effect? Does it renew you and encourage you to be generous and self-giving? Does it encourage self-absorption? What adjustments can you make so your ways of relaxing rejuvenate your spirit instead of draining it?

† In your immediate circle of influence, who is in need? What can you do to open yourself and pour out your gifts to help? Write two or three specific actions you will take this week to love in that way.

† Find a bouquet of your favorite flowers—buy one or make one—and keep it somewhere visible throughout this week. When you see it, stop and gaze at its beauty, drink in its aroma and its message: *True love means opening up the treasures of our life and sharing them with those in need.*

Chapter 4: *Humility*

Spring storms are wild. They can combine the angry bite of winter with the splendor of high summer: violent winds, stinging sleet, sudden temperature fluctuations, glorious drama. But spring storms can boast of at least one thing neither winter nor summer storms have. They cleanse the landscape and prepare it for a fresh start. Spring storms are nature's way of doing the annual spring-cleaning.

After one of these wild weather rides, lawns are littered with dead tree branches, leftover leaves, and other debris that spent the winter crouched in hidden corners protected from decay, even entire saplings that simply weren't strong enough to survive and thrive. The heavy rains serve to polish up the panorama so that the coming blossoms will really shine.

For us, spring-cleaning is deep cleaning, and it gets us ready for what's to come. It refreshes our homes and our minds. Our lives tend to accumulate unnecessary articles and superfluous stuff—not to mention actual dirt and dust and grime. In order to keep our homes beautiful (even just livable), we have to periodically peer into the hidden corners, scrubbing and wiping and tossing out things we no longer have a use for.

The need our houses have for this is obvious, but we have just as real a need to do something similar in our relationships, responsibilities, and psyches. Relationships can get cluttered with half-acknowledged misunderstandings and baggage, just as closets can get cluttered with old clothes. Our lives can get cluttered with so many activities and commitments that our normal pace increases and increases until it becomes abnormally frenetic. Our true selves can get lost beneath all that clutter, and we spend day after day regretting we don't have enough time anymore.

To keep relationships healthy and fresh, and to keep our own psychological and physiological selves polished and clean, we need to scrub hard and toss clutter away. But how do we do it? Self-discipline and common sense can help a lot. We can do more than we realize when we actually decide. Sometimes the hardest part is just making that decision and getting started.

When I took my vows of poverty, chastity, and obedience and joined a religious order, my favorite activity was prayer. During the years when I was discerning my call to the priesthood and religious life, I just loved prayer. I wasn't very good at it, but I loved it nevertheless. I used to covet bits and shards of time when I could sneak into a church and sit in contemplation. I would always have a pile of books I was meditating on. I would make a point of taking walks with the Lord in order to let the beauty of his creation seep into my soul. Whenever I was able to make time for prayer, I felt great. I felt God's presence almost tangibly. I felt renewed and empowered; I felt I could conquer the world.

Then I entered the novitiate (the first period of formation in religious life). For the first couple of weeks I felt like I had entered heaven. Our schedule was designed to give us a chance to go deep spiritually and truly discern whether God was calling us or not. It was centered on prayer, with some study and a lot of physical work mixed in. For the first time in my life, my daily schedule reflected the desires of my heart. We had nearly five hours a day reserved for prayer of different types. What a grace! It was like a spiritual honeymoon.

Then, to my astonishment and deep confusion, the honeymoon ended. After about six weeks, prayer became a burden. It became dry, difficult, even painful. I felt like I was being buffeted by the wild storms of early spring and no matter where I turned I couldn't find peace, only more wind and sleet and violent floods. I couldn't figure it out. I loved prayer! I had always palpably felt the presence of God in prayer. What was happening? Why was it that what had always been my refuge and my oasis had now become an exhausting, harsh wilderness in perpetual agitation?

This was the beginning of a long road of purification, of interior cleansing in which God showed me, gently but firmly, that my spiritual life was actually self-centered. If I wanted to be a priest of the Lord's kingdom, that had to change. He had sent me a spring storm to start cleaning out the dead and rotting corners of my soul that were out of my reach.

This is how we have to view hardship. God can handle it and will use it to lead us into a new springtime of spiritual fruitfulness. One of the best-known lines in the New Testament sums it up like this: "We know that all things work for good for those who love God, who are called according to his purpose" (Romans 8:28). If we are humble enough to accept our limitations and our need for grace, to realize that we are not God and that his providence surpasses our small abilities and enhances our sincere but inadequate efforts, then we won't panic or rebel when storms come our way. We will wait them out with confidence and look for the dead branches and decaying debris they stir up, sweep them away, and start fresh.

This is not to say that God is responsible for or directly wills all the storms that come through. God never wills moral evil, and moral evil—sin in all its forms—stirs up plenty of storms. God would prefer to avoid those storms, and many times he intervenes in hidden ways to protect us from them. We will only know how many storms we have been protected from when we reach our heavenly home. But we can't deny that God does permit evil and suffering in the world. He even threw himself into the middle of it when he became one of us through the Incarnation and suffered the terrible storm of betrayal and injustice that led to Jesus' condemnation, flagellation, and crucifixion.

The message of the Gospel and the message hidden in nature's springtime storms is that even the suffering caused by sin and evil can be redeemed. God's love is that powerful.

Saint Peter learned this lesson the hard way. We are all familiar with his sad story. He professed utter loyalty to Jesus, but Jesus knew him well and predicted that Peter would betray him. And that's what happened. Intimidated by some of the guards working for Jesus' enemies, Peter denied his Lord three times before the rooster crowed. He betrayed the one person he loved more than anyone else. He betrayed his own God and king, his own friend, his Savior. In so doing, he also betrayed himself. It was the absolute lowest point of his life, his most hideous failure. It is said that he wept for that betrayal every day for the rest of his life.

And yet even the interior storm caused by that dreadful sin became an instrument of redemption. After rising again from the dead, Jesus appeared to Peter and renewed their friendship, along with Peter's role as the leader of the other Twelve Apostles. It was precisely through his failure and the pain it caused that Peter learned the depth of Jesus' mercy and was given the strength to abandon his deeply embedded tendency to arrogant self-sufficiency once and for all.

Some of the dead branches and leaves that clutter our lives are out of our reach. No matter how hard we try to scrub up certain relationships or put the complex skeins of our responsibilities and commitments in order, we run up against our limits. That's where we can learn from the spring storms.

The winds and slashing rains of those storms reach every corner, cleansing in mere moments what a gardener could never reach even in as many months. These storms are necessary for nature to fulfill its potential, and the same is true for us. Some of the storms that hit our lives— explosive conflicts, agonizing losses, humiliating failures—are meant to cleanse us. They are meant to reach into the corners of our lives and purify what we could never clean up on our own. They are meant to reveal unhealthy branches in our own personalities that need to be cut away, and dead and decaying attitudes that are hiding in corners. Some storms, some crises, are necessary to help us discover, address, and deal with issues that are holding us back from flourishing. To allow those storms to do their work, as painful as it may be, all we need is humility.

Making It Your Own

† Choose one sentence from this chapter that really resonated in your heart or compose a one-sentence summary. Write it on a sticky note. Put it where you will see it throughout the week as a reminder that spring storms have a cleansing and purifying purpose.

† Take time this week to make a list of everything going on in your life, and then do some spring-cleaning. Ask yourself which of those commitments, activities, duties, and so on are essential and which are clutter. Then get rid of the clutter.

† Sign up for a weekend retreat during the coming year. Look around for a retreat center within driving distance that offers good, solid spiritual retreats. *Sign up.* Clear away the clutter from your schedule to make time for this. Give the Lord a weekend to speak to you about how much he loves you and what his hopes for you are this coming year.

† Identify any spring storms that may be happening in your life right now. What are their causes? What are you learning about yourself through them? What might God's providence be teaching you? Write the thoughts that come to mind, and then write down how you will handle those storms this week.

† The next time a big spring storm happens (a physical, weather storm), stop what you are doing, put on some galoshes and a big raincoat, and go out into it. Immerse yourself in it. Feel it. Get drenched. Watch the sheets of rain bash against everything and the gutters fill up and overflow and the trees bend to their breaking point. Enjoy it the way you used to when you were a child. And then enjoy the clean calm that comes afterward. Write a description of that experience and reread it the next time you find yourself in a life storm.

† This week, make an effort to exercise the virtue of humility. You can do this by verbally admitting when you don't know something instead of trying to cover up your ignorance. You can do it by accepting people's criticism without defending yourself. You can do it by going beyond the strict requirements of duty without looking for anything in return. Look ahead at your activities and commitments this week and try to discern where you may have chances to do those things.

Chapter 5: *Loyalty*

Herbaceous perennials play a key role in the glorious effervescence of spring. These plants rise up from the muddy soil with gusto every year, flowering and growing and spreading exuberantly during the warmer seasons. Then in the autumn they die back and seem to completely disappear in winter. But that's only an impression—a deceptive impression. In truth, they haven't disappeared at all. Their rootstock has simply taken refuge deep in the soil, waiting for the right time to branch out anew. You don't need to reseed flowers like asters, coneflowers, and bluebells when they grow in their native climate. They stay the course and blossom every year no matter how harsh the winter may have been. They are perennials. You can count on them, as you can count on spring itself.

Some people are like perennials. You can count on them. You know they won't abandon or betray you. Even if you don't see them or speak to them for a long while, as soon as you get back in touch it's just like it was before—no complications, no misunderstandings, no resentments. These are the perennials in human relationships, the loyal ones.

We all need loyal friends. We all need people in our lives who can put up with our flaws and failings and still stay the course. We need friends who know how to take refuge in the deeper soil of our sincere esteem and devotion during the wintery moments when our selfishness gets the better of us. We all need perennials.

I got in a fight once when I was a kid. It wasn't an elegant and noble fight. I took advantage of someone who was weaker than me and imposed my will on him. It was shameful. And as I walked home from the bus stop I quickly realized and felt just how shameful it was. I knew the other kid's parents would soon find out about it, and word would reach my dad. And my dad wasn't going to be pleased. He had been a professional boxer for a while and had taught my sisters and me how to fight. He wanted us to be able to defend ourselves, not to become bullies. I was going to be in trouble.

During the walk home, I contemplated my options. I think I considered running away. I also considered going back to the other kid and offering to bribe him with a candy bar so he wouldn't tell on me. But I knew in my heart that it was too late for any of that. So I decided to take the bull by the horns and turn myself in.

As soon as my dad got home I went right up to him and told him what had happened. As I confessed the ugly truth, I started to cry, and by the end of my monologue I was a sobbing mess, running to my room before my dad could say anything in response. I threw myself onto my bed and buried my face in my pillow, wallowing in my sorrow and shame.

I don't remember how long I stayed there, but eventually I heard a knock on my door. My dad came in and sat on my bed. He put his hand on my shoulder and started talking. He was calm and relaxed, which really surprised me. I thought he would be angry. He told me that what I did was wrong, ugly, and unworthy. He told me that he was disappointed in me for doing it. But then he said that I had done the right thing by coming and telling him, by not trying to hide from the truth or cover it up. He said that he was proud of me for owning up to my failure and taking responsibility for it.

As he transitioned into this praise and appreciation, I blinked my eyes and wiped away the tears. I stared at him as he talked and felt myself being rejuvenated and energized. I had failed, but I wasn't a failure. I had messed up, but that wasn't the last chapter of the story. At the end of the encounter, he gave me a hug and then pulled out his wallet and handed me an extra allowance as a reward for doing the right thing after doing the wrong thing.

I think that was my first experience of mercy—at least, it's the first one I remember. It was the first time I consciously recognized that I didn't deserve to be loved or trusted anymore, but someone continued to love and trust me anyway. Someone was loyal to me. Someone popped through the soil of my sorrow like a Peruvian lily and gave new life to my winterized soul. I never got into another fight again.

The rootstock of loyalty is mercy. We all mess up; we all have meltdown moments when we say and do things we later regret, things that hurt other people. We don't really *deserve* to be forgiven for those outbursts. They were wrong and we should have controlled ourselves better. But that's why mercy is so important. Mercy forgives when we don't really deserve to be forgiven. It gives us a fresh start. It gives us a new springtime.

For someone to be a loyal perennial in our lives, he needs to be merciful. And if we're not willing to be that way, we will eventually undermine all of our relationships, trapping ourselves in an emotional and spiritual isolation chamber of our own making. Only loneliness, frustration, and despair will accompany us there. Without the refreshing and inspiring loveliness of perennials popping up in the messy soil of early spring, we can't find the strength to leave behind our winters.

We need to be grateful for the perennials that give spring its first color and song. We need to be grateful for the loyal friends who bring springtimes of mercy into our lives. The flower of loyalty and its rootstock of mercy are essential elements of a fulfilling and fruitful life.

But we also need to realize that we can *be* those loyal friends. Almost on a daily basis we have chances to forgive and affirm people. Human beings mess up. That's part of who we are. We should never condone the mess-ups or enable the dysfunctions, but we can and must forgive and affirm. "Blessed are the merciful," Jesus taught in an age before mercy was valued at all, "for they will be shown mercy" (Matthew 5:7). And another of his favorite things to say was, "Your sins are forgiven …go in peace" Luke 7:48, 50).

In our digital society, the world needs loyalty and mercy more than ever before. People's failures and flaws are broadcast farther and wider now than was even imaginable just a few decades ago. And they are never erased. The digital world is unforgetting, and too often also unforgiving. Once someone is given a scarlet letter, once someone is labeled one way or another, it becomes part of that person's profile and sticks wherever they go.

Most of us have experienced the pain that comes with that dynamic. But perhaps we have also experienced the relief that comes from experiencing loyalty, from encountering the much deeper truth of mercy. And we can all choose to be oases of loyalty and springtides of mercy. By allowing ourselves to experience the unconditional acceptance and forgiveness that Jesus is always ready to offer us—either directly through prayer and the sacraments or indirectly through the loyalty of our friends—we can accept others in the same way. We can break through the harsh winter of our one-and-done culture and pour forth the beauty and fragrance of a spiritual spring.

God is the creator of perennials. He envisioned their DNA and joyfully planted them in this world of spinning winters and wild springtimes. God is also the author of mercy, the most loyal friend and companion we could ever imagine. He wants to be our primary perennial. Let's give him the chance.

Making It Your Own

† Choose one sentence from this chapter that really resonated in your heart or compose a one-sentence summary. Write it on a sticky note. Put it where you will see it throughout the week as a reminder to be grateful for the perennials in your life and follow their example in how you treat others.

† What have been your most intense and memorable experiences of loyalty and mercy? This week, take time to write them down, describing them in detail. Remember them, relive them, savor them, thank God for them.

† Who are the perennials (people, not flowers) in your life right now? Spend time with one of them this week and tell the person how much you appreciate his or her loyalty to you.

† Who in your circle of influence is in need of a fresh start right now? In need of an act of merciful loyalty? Take time to identify someone in particular. Reflect on how you can reach out to that individual this week and be his or her perennial. Make a commitment to do so. Put it in your calendar to help you remember.

† Do some research about perennial flowers. Find out which ones would grow best in your climate, then get some. Plant them where you'll be able to see them year after year. If you have nowhere to plant them, learn to recognize them. Then, whenever you see them, let them remind you of the importance and power of loyalty, and say a prayer of thanksgiving to God for bringing mercy into the world.

† Take time this week to read and reflect on Jesus' most famous parable, a parable of mercy, the parable of the Prodigal Son. You will find it in your Bible in chapter 15 of Luke's Gospel. Get out your Bible now and put a bookmark there so you can read and reflect on the story later, in a moment of calm and quiet.

Chapter 6: *Patience*

Spring is a transition. It's an in-between season whose identity shares characteristics of both winter and summer. Some days it feels like the end of winter, other days it feels like the beginning of summer. And it's messy. The wintry days don't all happen first and the summery days don't all happen second. They get mixed up. You get a few clear and bright and warm days that make you think winter is finally over, and then it snows again. You put on your light spring jacket one day, and two days later you have to bundle up in winter coats and scarves and gloves. That's how transition periods are: messy, rough, unpredictable, uncomfortable. Even the smoothest transition isn't really smooth, just relatively so.

Truly seeing this characteristic of spring—noticing it, contemplating it, meditating on it, thinking deeply about it, understanding it, accepting it—can help equip us to manage our own life transitions more elegantly. And we really need that help because our post-modern world has lost a lot of ground in this area.

Advanced technology purposely tries to minimize transition times. Having what we want as soon as possible and with as little trouble as possible is a watchword for technological progress. When a machine takes too much time to start, or when we have to wait around for it to get warmed up, we get frustrated and angry; we lose patience. We think that if something takes a lot of time we're doing it wrong.

But that's not true. Going from winter to summer takes time. It's supposed to take time. That's how nature works. Nothing is wrong with that. In fact, spring is part of the natural rhythm of our universe, and God created that rhythm with us in mind, to give us a proper habitat for growing and flourishing, physically, emotionally, and spiritually.

Human beings are not machines. We are living creatures of a wise and powerful Creator. Our human nature has its rhythms. We go through transitions that shouldn't be rushed, that can't be rushed. And so our most human endeavors also have a rhythm and go through periods of transition. Even the research and development that eventually created those advanced technologies had its ups and downs and went through a lot of stages.

❦

How do you feel when impatience gets in the driver's seat of your consciousness? You feel stressed, angry, high-strung, anxious. You lose objectivity and start saying and doing things that end up making the situation worse, maybe even leaving a trail of human wreckage in your wake. Impatience is a gear that strips our transmissions raw. It was the tortoise that won the race—slow and steady, patient and persistent—not the explosive hare.

Patience enables us to keep our cool in upsetting and dysfunctional situations. It enables us to be productive and wise when our spontaneous, impatient reactions would lead us to be destructive and imprudent. Patience gives us the insight to recognize when we are in the midst of a transition, and to work fruitfully within the limitations that go along with that.

I remember a particularly challenging transition I had to go through in my years of preparation for the priesthood. After my fourth year of seminary formation, my religious superiors assigned me to join a team of priests who were to serve as translators for an international retreat for clergy sponsored by the Vatican. The retreat was part of the Church's preparation to celebrate the Great Jubilee of the Year 2000. It was scheduled to take place in the summer in a Catholic shrine in the Ivory Coast. I had never been to Africa and was excited and nervous about the opportunity.

The experience proved to be intense and enriching. Thousands of priests from all over the world participated. Our simultaneous translation work was grueling, but we also had bits and pieces of free time when we were able to go out and experience local life. It was an eye-opening cultural experience in many ways and a particularly valuable one for a young seminarian.

When I left Africa to return to my seminary community, I was elated and exhausted. I had a lot that I needed to process, but I didn't really understand that. And so, when I got home I thought I could just nonchalantly re-enter the normal swing of things. It didn't work. Without knowing why, I became extremely volatile. I found myself bouncing dangerously between intense highs and lows, and I had no idea why.

At one point, I was speaking with my spiritual director about it. I read to him some paragraphs I had written in my spiritual journal about what I was feeling. He was so shocked by what I read that it made him doubt my vocation to the priesthood. He told me that maybe I was feeling this way because I wasn't called to be a priest.

That was a seismic shock to me. I had never doubted my call. I spent the next three days in the chapel, desperately praying for guidance instead of following the normal seminary schedule.

Those three days of quiet prayer and reflection were exactly what I needed. In a sense, the desperation sparked by my spiritual director's comments forced me out of my normal activities and gave me the space I needed to transition back into ordinary life after my turbulent mission trip to Africa. I hadn't given myself the time I needed. It was my first real, lived lesson in the importance of patience during times of transition.

A crucial spiritual principle is involved with this need for patience in transition, a principle eloquently explained by St. Ignatius of Loyola.

Ignatius was an unlikely saint. He entered adulthood as a minor nobleman and knight in fifteenth century Spain. He was hot-blooded and impulsive, and loved all the pomp and passing glory of worldly affairs. All that changed when he was severely injured during a battle. He was confined to bed for months. During that time he ended up reading biographies of saints.

This period of forced rest became a season of grace for the fiery military man. He heard God's call in his heart and changed the course of his life. He decided to become a missionary, turning his martial skills and zeal in a spiritual direction. He ended up founding one of the most influential and fruitful religious orders in the Catholic Church, the Society of Jesus, also known as the Jesuits.

At the core of his spiritual experience was what he called discernment. He emphasized the importance of learning to read what is going on inside our own souls so we can become adept at identifying the origin of different inspirations, desires, and feelings. Some of those come from our own self, some come from the Holy Spirit who tries to guide us to true happiness, and some come from the enemy of every human soul, the devil and his demons, who try to lead us away from friendship with God.

Saint Ignatius wrote a book called *The Spiritual Exercises* in which he develops his ideas on discernment. He provides "rules for the discernment of spirits" that can help spiritual directors, as well as everyone else, learn to see more clearly what is going on in our souls.

One of these rules is especially applicable to times of transition. This rule warns against reversing decisions made in periods of clarity and calm when those periods give way to times of turbulence. The idea is simple. In the midst of calm and clarity, we see things more objectively and have a better chance of making prudent decisions. In times of turbulence, our vision is obstructed and our emotions are agitated. It's the worst time to reevaluate and redirect. We need to stay the course and wait for calm and clarity to return. We need to be patient.

That's a great rule of thumb for times of transition. Moving to a new city and a new job, for example, is a time of transition, full of pains and difficulties of every order. In the midst of that chaotic and challenging period of change, we should be very suspicious of thoughts that come uninvited into our minds and suggest that we throw in the towel and go back to the way things were before. The decision to move was made in a time of calm and clarity, with lots of reflection and discussion. To change it or question it during the necessary turbulence that accompanies the demanding process of transitioning would be unwise.

The same principle can also be applied to other types of transitions. When we end a relationship for good reasons, we should be patient with ourselves during the immediate aftermath, humbly acknowledging that we are going to be in an emotionally vulnerable state for a season, and so we should avoid making any major commitments for a while. When a couple gets married, the first years will be years of major, radical transition, with wintry days and summery days. Questioning the commitment during that turbulent springtime will usually not bring lasting peace. When we lose a loved one, we can't expect to be indifferent to the loss. A season of transition will follow, for a longer or shorter duration depending on many factors outside of our control, when we need to exercise a lot of patience and avoid rash decisions. Some sicknesses require months or even years of recovery —a long transition back to health. In all these cases, and in so many more, we need to give ourselves time.

❦

God knew what he was doing when he inserted spring between winter and summer. The seasonal transition, with all its ups and downs, with all its reverses and dramatic identity troubles, is an integral part of nature. It takes time to make that transition, and that's OK.

Just so, the transitions that life requires of us take time. They are natural processes that unfold gradually and organically, with plenty of uncomfortable and even violent turbulence. That's OK. That's the way we are created. We just need to be patient. And with God's help, we can.

Making It Your Own

† Choose one sentence from this chapter that really resonated in your heart or compose a one-sentence summary. Write it on a sticky note. Put it where you will see it throughout the week as a reminder that you're not a piece of advanced technology and some of your transitions will take time and require patience.

† Take time this week to sit down and reflect on the biggest transitions in your life. Describe them to yourself in detail, maybe writing those descriptions in a journal. Use this exercise to grow in wisdom, self-awareness, and self-knowledge. How did those transitions make you feel? What were their challenges and opportunities? How did you react to them? What patterns emerge regarding how you generally deal with transitions? What did you learn from them? What would you do differently if you could live them over again?

† Make a list of the things, situations, and people that typically trigger your impatience. Then think deeply about why they do so. What does this tell you about yourself? What will you do about it?

† What transition are you going through right now? Take time this week to stop and think about it. What is it demanding of you? How are you handling it? If you were a bit more patient with it, what would that look like and how would it affect your daily living?

† Think about the people in your circle of influence who are undergoing major transitions. Brainstorm how you could help support them in that process. Come up with at least ten ideas, then take the three that resonate with you most deeply and commit to doing them. Write them in your calendar to help you remember.

† Write a poem or make a drawing (or other artwork) titled "Transitions." Then write/ make another one titled "Patience." Compare the two. Reflect on what they reveal to you about yourself. Speak to God about that in prayer.

Chapter 7: *Responsibility*

Spring is a planting season. Farmers have to act fast once spring breaks. They have to read the weather and identify the small window in which they can plant their crops—after the last frost and after the heaviest rains that would wash away or flood new seeds. Then they have to do the actual planting by plowing the soil, fertilizing, laying the seed, irrigating, and preparing all the tools and materials necessary for this complex and delicate process.

Reading the weather takes keen observation and practical wisdom. Planting the seed takes hard work. If farmers are careless on either point, the entire growing season will suffer because of it, their economy will be severely strained, and the consequences will reverberate into daily struggles for the whole family during the next winter. They need to be responsible in order to be fruitful.

Who would you rather have: a responsible, hard-working teammate or an undependable, lazy one? The answer is obvious. And yet, when it comes down to it, many people have trouble being responsible. We know what we should do, but we hem and haw about it. We procrastinate, like a teenager who spends twice as much energy finding ways to avoid his chores than simply doing them.

Irresponsibility may seem like a minor fault, but it isn't. Habits of carelessness and irresponsibility breed other bad habits. We end up learning to deceive and lie to cover up our shortcomings. We end up violating justice by causing other people to suffer the consequences of our neglect, forcing them to pick up our slack. We end up becoming slaves of our feelings and our whims, eager to indulge in what pleases us and allergic to the productive and truly fulfilling demands of meaningful work.

Habits of laziness lead us to betray what really matters to us because we can no longer muster the self-discipline and self-control required to care for them. Picture the couch-potato dad who has become entirely disengaged from the lives of his wife and children. Picture the superficial country-clubber who squanders all her life-giving creativity in petty gossip and social intrigue. Picture the twenty-something guy who spends seven hours a day playing video games—his virtual reality stealing the best years of his life.

When I was in college, one of my on-campus jobs was showing slides for art history lectures. (This was before the advent of easily manageable computer presentation programs.) The art history professors would arrange their photo slides in order, then, during the lecture, I would sit in the projection booth and insert each slide into the projector at the proper time. When the professor pressed a button on his lectern, a red light would go on to indicate that I needed to project the next slide. It was labor intensive, but it worked pretty well—as long as the guy in the projector booth was on the ball.

I prided myself on being good at it. I was super-responsible. I always showed up early and paid fabulously strict attention during the lectures, even trying to anticipate when the next slide would be needed. My performance was even recognized by the head of the department, who started giving me special assignments.

One of these was scheduled for a Saturday morning. A world-renowned lecturer was scheduled to give a presentation to an annual gathering of experts in his field. The experts were flying in from all over the country and beyond. This lecture was the first of a full day's congress, and it was meant to set the tone for the rest of the activities. I was to be in charge of the projection booth. And since it was a Saturday morning and no one else would be around, I was given the key to open the booth.

As a college sophomore, I treasured my weekends. Staying up late, sleeping in, hanging out, relaxing....That weekend I treasured my free time a little too much. I stayed up late on Friday night and completely forgot about the Saturday-morning lecture. To be honest, when I finally did open my eyes long after the sun had risen, I had a vague feeling that I was supposed to be somewhere. But it was *so* vague that I dismissed it in favor of a luxurious morning of self-indulgence.

No one was there to open the projection booth and show the slides. No one was in the office to call me to remind me of my duty. The world-renowned lecturer had nowhere to turn. His lecture was ruined. The long flights of the 200 experts were for naught. They all had to settle for a simple verbal description of the slides that I could not project because I was still snoring. I failed to perform my simple, mundane duty, just because of a fairly innocent bout of carelessness, and the entire event went up in smoke (which I heard about in great detail the following Monday). Just like that. Such is the power of irresponsibility.

This is one of the funny things about being human. We have the capacity to be responsible and irresponsible. Ants don't. Squirrels don't. Their instincts guide them invariably to do what they need to do in order to survive. You can never blame them for being lazy or careless. Their internal programming takes care of them.

Not so with people. We have instincts, but we also have minds and creative freedom. Our programming—God's design for our human nature—includes free will. That includes our ability to think and decide things for ourselves. We are cocreators with God. God built the mountains; we build cathedrals. God paints the sunsets; we paint portraits, write great novels, and make beautiful movies. Our human spirit is not limited to instinct; it includes freedom.

This spiritual dimension God has woven into us enables us to be creative and to imagine God in this world much more gloriously than even the cutest squirrel. But it also opens up the possibility of distorting the image of God. No squirrel can rebel against its "squirrel-ness." No tree can foolishly uproot itself from the soil because it wants to wander around the forest like a raccoon. Human beings can. We can rebel against our nature, silencing the voice of conscience and disobeying the laws given to our nature in order to guide us to fulfillment. This rebellion is called sin. And one of its most common manifestations is laziness, slothfulness, indolence: simple irresponsibility.

Our duties are the primary arena in which we can show our love. A mother has certain duties in relation to her children. A husband has certain duties in relation to his wife. An employee and a boss have certain duties toward each other, toward the company they work for, and the people that company serves. Elected officials have certain duties in regard to the people who elected them. A priest has certain duties in relation to the Church and its members. Every human person, merely by being human, has duties to God and neighbor. These duties are beautiful things!

In a sense, our duties define us. They set the parameters for how we, as unique individuals, are called to make our mark in this world. They show us, at least in part, where we should go and how to get there. They are invitations that we have the ability to respond to; they reflect our humanness, our response-ability.

The farmer doesn't look at spring with dread. He doesn't turn away from the window of opportunity for planting. He doesn't regret that he has to get out and get to work. Without a doubt, his work is demanding and tiring, but it is *his* work; it is *his* responsibility; and fulfilling that responsibility is part of how he sees God in the world. We should all learn a lesson from that example and realize that the duties and responsibilities that flow from our place and relationships here on earth are as much a part of God's beautiful plan for our lives as the thaws and rains of springtime.

We all want the responsible, hard-working person on our team. So let's recommit ourselves to *being* that responsible, hard-working person. When it's time to plant, let's role up our sleeves and plant. Only then will we be able to truly enjoy the harvest.

Making It Your Own

† Choose one sentence from this chapter that really resonated in your heart or compose a one-sentence summary. Write it on a sticky note. Put it where you will see it throughout the week as a reminder of the value of hard work and the consequences of laziness.

† Take time to reflect on the most common manifestations of laziness in your life. Remember that laziness is not the same as taking a reasonable amount of time for necessary, healthy rest and relaxation. Laziness has to do with shirking responsibility, cutting corners, procrastinating, and so on. How does sloth show up in your life? Why?

† Make a list of all your roles and relationships (work, family, Church, and so on). Now give

yourself a grade for your level of responsibility in each of those relationships. Choose one of the lower-graded relationships and make a list of three things you can do to be more responsible in it. Commit to doing at least one of those things this week. Put it on your calendar to help you remember.

† Identify three people you have somehow hurt, whether they realize it or not, through moments of irresponsibility. Make a list of what you could do to make it up to them—directly or indirectly. Choose one of those things and commit to doing it this week. Put it on your calendar to help you remember.

† The duties we have to ourselves and to God, just because we are human beings, are summed up in what is called the moral law, or the law of human nature. These appear in the Bible under the Ten Commandments. Take time this week to find and go over a good examination of conscience based on the Ten Commandments.[2] Be thorough and honest. Then go to confession to confess your faults and sins and make a fresh start.

---

[2] A good example is available online from the Catholic Diocese of Arlington, VA: arlingtondiocese.org/documents/worship_examconscience.pdf

† Sometimes lazy behavior that occurs only in certain sectors of our lives can be linked to deeper issues than simple irresponsibility. It may be a sign that we have some unhealed emotional wounds or that we have made some wrong choices we need to reevaluate. Take time this week to meet with a mentor, spiritual director, or other wise person you trust to talk about some of the habits in your life you aren't happy about. Ask this person to help you uncover possible hidden causes and suggestions on what you should do next.

Chapter 8: *Wisdom*

Springtime usually has connotations of freshness, energy, and enthusiasm, but that's not how we tend to think of wisdom. We tend to associate wisdom with age and experience, while spring is the season of youth and inexperience. If we look with care though, we can see spring does have its own wisdom. Maybe, in a certain sense, all the other chapters of this book could be taken as an expression of springtime's wisdom. That would be a general treatment, but springtime has a specific wisdom, too.

Spring's contribution to wisdom can be summed up like this: *New beginnings are always possible.* Spring is a new season, a fresh and bright season. And no matter how cold and long the winter, spring always follows; it always begins again.

Wisdom has to do with knowledge in action. Professors and intellectuals can have an abundance of knowledge, but unless that knowledge has helped them learn the art of living, we don't call them wise. An uneducated peasant may have less book knowledge, but if the knowledge that such a person gleans from nature and from life reaches not only his mind but his heart, he may be wiser than any professor. The wise person knows how to interpret events and how to make the right decision in difficult circumstances. When you need advice, you go to someone who is wise.

Like spring, we also can begin again. Failure is never final in this life or on this beautiful, God-given earth. We can always have a fresh start. The circumstances will be different. The losses from what passed before are real and we can't ignore them or pretend they don't hurt. The damage from winter is true damage. But even so, we can always begin again.

My first lessons in new beginnings came from my dad. He possessed this wisdom of springtime. He taught it to me both through his example and by his words.

When I was five years old, my parents separated and then divorced. My mother was ill, but my dad didn't know it. Her illness contributed to their breakup, though no one knew it at the time. She died when I was nine. This failed marriage was my dad's biggest regret in life. He always thought that if he had only known my mom was sick they would have been able to stay together.

He never had a chance for a new beginning with her. Soon after the divorce, he married again, feeling that my two sisters and I really needed a mom in the house, but that relationship failed quickly. We had to move to temporary housing for a few months before my dad was able to find a new home for us—yet another new beginning.

Those were unstable years. And yet, Dad always kept looking for a fresh start. He never tired of trying to make it work, of making as many new beginnings as necessary. In the throes of post-modern family life, he showed me the wisdom of springtime.

The wisdom of spring is the wisdom of the pioneer, of the inventor, of the adventurer. Things rarely work out perfectly the first time. Inventors know that. Thomas Edison once quipped that genius is 1 percent inspiration and 99 percent perspiration. In order to find the right material for the first commercialized electric light bulb, he and his collaborators had to begin again more than 6,000 times. Things didn't work out perfectly the first time; they had to keep starting over, and over, and over.

Pioneers have this wisdom, too. The men and women who left the comforts of home in order to go west during the great period of expansion in nineteenth-century America knew that. They moved on, settled down, and often had to move on again, and again, and even again. But eventually those covered wagons reached their destination, and one or two log cabins soon multiplied into a settlement, then a town, a city, an entire state.

Those pioneers were following in the footsteps of the pilgrims, the first Europeans to settle on the North American coast, spurred on by the conviction that it was time to leave the Old World behind and begin again. They believed in the possibility of starting over.

Certainly we don't want to canonize every pilgrim and every pioneer—they were sinners, just like the rest of us. But neither should we deny that we are the beneficiaries of the new culture they formed. The American spirit has irrefutably made a contribution to the world, to the history of the human family. And that contribution flowed from the wisdom those pioneers showed in living out their conviction that new beginnings are always possible.

We are all, in some way or another, pilgrims and pioneers. The human spirit resonates with the conviction that new beginnings are always possible, a truth woven into the most native rhythms of life on earth. Allow this truth to penetrate not only your mind but also your heart. New beginnings are always possible, even right here and right now.

We have all heard the schoolchild's dictum: "If at first you don't succeed, try, try again." And yet, has this really become wisdom for us, or has it remained merely at the level of knowledge, of trivia? Are we convinced that new beginnings are always possible? Have we truly listened to the lesson springtime wants to teach us?

As many times as we fail, we can begin again. Tradition tells us that Jesus stumbled and fell multiple times as he carried his cross to Calvary, and he got up every time and continued forward. So can we. He fell and got up again so we would know how to do the same. We will always have falls, but we can always get up again and continue forward.

This applies not only to projects and endeavors but also to relationships and personal growth. If we want to grow in patience, it doesn't matter how many times we fall into impatience. We can always begin again. God's grace will help us. If we want to spend time in prayer every day but keep failing in our resolution, we can keep trying new ways to make it work. Some broken or dysfunctional relationships need to be left behind and entrusted to God's mercy, but that doesn't mean that we can't have meaningful and beautiful new relationships in the future. And when we hurt those we love, we can always humble ourselves and ask for forgiveness and begin again.

Making It Your Own

† Choose one sentence from this chapter that really resonated in your heart or compose a one-sentence summary. Write it on a sticky note. Put it where you will see it throughout the week as a reminder spring is not just about youthful excitement but also has its wisdom.

† When have you made a fresh start? What have been your most powerful new beginnings? Take time this week to reflect back on them, maybe even looking over old pictures or visiting old places. Let the experiences you have had nourish your conviction and increase your wisdom.

† Take time this week to go through the aspects of your life that you may have given up on or become cynical about. Reflect calmly on each of them. How can you apply the wisdom of new beginnings to them? Is it a question of accepting that they are truly over and moving on to something new? Or are there some aspects that you should revisit, redeem, and revitalize? Pray about this and ask God to show you the wise path to follow.

† What avenue do you have in your life for expressing the pioneer spirit? Take time this week to stir up this spirit and allow the freshness of springtime to reawaken your creativity.

† Think about the people in your life. Is anyone struggling to make a new beginning? How can you help him or her do this? Commit to giving the help you can this week, even if it's only an encouraging word over a cup of coffee. Put it on your calendar to help you remember.

† Take time this week to create a personal symbol of new beginnings. Make a drawing or a painting, write a poem, design a meme, erect a monument. Find a way to assimilate this lesson and make it meaningful to you personally.

Chapter 9: *Discernment*

The landscape explodes with renewed life in springtime. The earth produces a wildly abundant variety of plants—dozens of types of trees, scores of species of flowers, a dizzying variety of ground cover. Each of these carries its particular identity deep within itself, but the full expression of that identity blossoms under the influence of all the other common springtime elements: sunlight, soil, water, air, and warmth. Those elements are generic. They don't change. They are the basic requirements for growth. Yet they produce an almost infinite variety of living beings. The same sunlight, soil, water, and air releases the hidden potential of maple trees and cedar trees, roses and rhododendrons, ivy and irises, dandelions and dogwoods. The unique identity of each natural species flourishes under the influence of the most mundane and common natural elements.

Something similar happens in the spiritual realm. Each one of us is created to reflect God's grandeur in a unique way. Each of us can know and love

God—who is infinite—in an absolutely unique way. No one in the history of the universe can repeat you. No one. No one can come to love God as you do. No one will know God just as you will come to know him. Each of us is a particular story unfolding in matchless complexity. This is what it means to be a spiritual person and not just a material thing.

The elements that must be present for us to reach the full expression of our identity are common: a family or intimate community of some sort; food, shelter, and clothing; loving attention from parents and the education that flows from their love; a wider society and the cultural milieu it creates; prayer and spiritual nourishment. Throw any human being into that environment and a unique person will emerge.

But it's possible for our development to be frustrated. We are not fully determined by our DNA, as daffodils and oak trees are. As spiritual beings, we have to cooperate consciously with our own development. We have to make choices about how we will respond to the different influences at work around us and how we will invest our natural talents. If we allow ourselves to be overly influenced by others, our personal identity will never fully thrive. If those others are morally corrupt, we may even be wounded or thwarted in our quest for meaning and happiness. If we make unwise use of our God-given abilities and talents, we will impede our development and hinder our flourishing, just like plants that need sunlight get scrawny when stuck in the shade.

How can we make the right decisions? How can we respond prudently to the influences around us, taking advantage of the good opportunities and steering clear of the dead ends? How can we invest our talents fruitfully, avoiding frustration and regret? It takes *discernment*.

I remember one dead end that I was stuck in as a boy, and once again it was my dad who helped me get out of it. He gave me my first lesson in discernment when I was blinded by a failure.

When I was in fifth grade, a teacher told me about the annual sixth-grade speech contest. Every year sixth-graders could compete in this contest by memorizing and delivering the Gettysburg Address. The winner was given the privilege of reciting it at the town's annual Memorial Day Celebration in the village cemetery. As soon as I heard about it, I was determined to win it.

I bought a large poster of the whole Gettysburg Address and put it up on my bedroom wall. I began to memorize it more than a year before the contest. I just loved it. I looked up all the words and knew what they all meant. I became a big fan of Abraham Lincoln. My patriotism flourished. I was determined to win this contest and play a role in these events.

But then, on the contest day, I stumbled. I messed up the last line of the Gettysburg Address. And so I came in second place. I was devastated. I wouldn't even talk to the girl who won—I couldn't! The social studies teacher tried to comfort me, but I was inconsolable. He handed me a few sheets of paper with another famous speech written on it— Logan's Orders. The runner-up in the contest was granted the honor of reading that speech during the celebration. I took the papers without thinking and went home.

My dad found me in my bedroom, moping. I had failed. It was over. He tried to cheer me up, to no avail. Then he asked me what those papers were. I explained that I was supposed to read Logan's Orders at the ceremony, but it was no big deal, because I had lost the contest. He picked up the papers, read them over, and then he said, "This is a great speech. This may be almost as great as the Gettysburg Address, and it's longer. It's a longer speech." That piqued my interest a little bit. Then he looked me in the eye and said, "When are you going to get started?" I sat up and looked at him quizzically: "What do you mean? All I have to do is get up and read it when they call on me. What do I need to get started with?" And he said, "Well, I think you should memorize it. It's a great speech. It will be better if you memorize it." Shocked, I retorted, "But I don't have time. The ceremony is on Sunday." He paused, looked away, then handed me back the papers and said, "I think you can do it." Then he left the room and closed the door.

He had helped me see a new beginning in what I thought was a sad ending; he had helped me discern a fruitful path forward where I perceived only a dead end.

❧

The discerning person knows how to sift through all the possibilities and identify which ones are worthy and which ones aren't. Many principles go into healthy discernment. One of them comes to us from this reflection on the wide variety of species that explode under the influence of some basic, common elements.

Each type of flower possesses its core identity from within, not from without. The outer elements only allow the hidden center to expand and become what it is meant to be. The identity is in the seed, though its power to grow is released by the soil.

Likewise, God's dream for each person unfolds from within. We need to be true to what God has planted within our souls. To make good decisions and sift through all the possibilities and influences that swirl around us, we must learn to listen to his whispers in our hearts, to be true to our deeper selves.

This doesn't mean that outside influences are indifferent. Poison will kill a plant, but water will help it grow. If our true identity is to flourish, we must avoid spiritual poisons—they are called sins.

But when we are choosing between various good options, one key indicator that can help us discern which will be most helpful for us, for the unfolding of our unique story as God envisions it, is internal resonance. Certain possibilities make our hearts sing and trigger an interior dynamism; other ones seem to move us from the outside only, like an external pressure. It is not always easy to distinguish—we are very complex beings. And this isn't the only principle of discernment. But it's one we should learn to appreciate.

One of the most famous instances of this principle of discernment at work is linked to St. Anthony the Abbot, a third-century aristocrat who became the founder of Christian monasticism.

Anthony's parents died when he was only a young man, leaving him a huge inheritance— lands, houses, money, industries, a mountain of wealth. Everyone, including Anthony himself, thought he would spend the rest of his life enjoying and managing his family estate. It seemed clear. Who needed discernment to figure out something so obvious? God's dream for Anthony was different.

The future saint first began to discern his true path while he was listening to the Gospel passage at Mass. That day, some well-known words of Jesus struck a chord deep within his heart that they had never struck before. He heard the proclamation of Matthew 19:21: "If you wish to be perfect, go, sell what you have and give to [the] poor, and you will have treasure in heaven. Then come, follow me." He knew that those words were being spoken directly to him. He couldn't mistake the profound resonance they had; he was convinced that God was making that call reverberate in his heart. He obeyed what he heard, literally, giving away everything from his inheritance except what he and his sister needed to survive.

But he didn't stop there. Soon afterward, he heard other familiar words of the Lord proclaimed during the Mass: "Do not worry about tomorrow; tomorrow will take care of itself. Sufficient for a day is its own evil" (Matthew 6:34). Once again, those words resounded so powerfully in the depths of the soul that he knew the Lord was asking him to act on them in a radical way. He arranged for his younger sister to be provided for and then went into the desert with absolutely no possessions.

There he began his life as a monk, separated from the affairs of the world and dedicated to prayer, sacrifice, and spiritual warfare. With God's help, he was able to win victory after victory, fulfilling God's plan for his life. This not only flooded his own soul with joy and meaning but also, through the monastic movement that grew out of his obedience to God's call, it opened a wide channel of grace that has never since stopped flowing into the world.

God knew his dream for St. Anthony, and St. Anthony discovered and discerned it by attending to God's voice deep in his heart. Many other people were also present on those days when Anthony received his calling, and they heard the same words proclaimed. But Anthony's spiritual DNA reacted differently to them, because that's how God created him, and he successfully discerned how to respond.

Learning to hear the whisper of God deep within our souls requires a decision to dedicate time on a regular basis to personal reflection. As Plato put it many centuries ago, "the unexamined life is not worth living." We have to retreat from the noise and the busyness of our wild world on a regular basis and listen to what is happening in our heart. Then, gradually, we will learn to hear what God is saying to us and where his personal love for us is leading.

In earlier epochs—non-digital and non-mass media eras—doing so was easier than it is now. But that's no excuse. No one forces us to stay plugged in 24/7. No one forces us to dwell solely on the scintillating surface of news headlines, fads, and social media. We can unplug whenever we want, for however long we want. We can take time to build meaningful and profound relationships. We can make some quiet time dedicated to prayer and personal reflection for fifteen minutes every day, for half a day every week, for one day every couple months, for one weekend every year. We can learn to be deep and discerning, so our true identity can fully flourish. Why not start—or jump-start—right now?

Making It Your Own

† Choose one sentence from this chapter that really resonated in your heart or compose a one-sentence summary. Write it on a sticky note. Put it where you will see it throughout the week as a reminder that you have a unique identity, and discernment will help it to flourish.

† When have you felt most fulfilled in your life? Take time to reflect on those experiences or moments. Describe them in detail by writing them in a journal. Relive the feelings that they gave you. Sensitize yourself so as to recognize and embrace similar opportunities in the future.

† Which "common elements" (prayer, friendship, family, healthy food and rest, meaningful work) that every human being needs in order

to thrive are less present in your life than they should be? What can you do about that? What will you do about it this week?

† What influences and opportunities are at work in your life right now? Make a list of them. How are you responding to them? How confident are you that you are responding well? Identify two or three that you need to engage in intentional discernment about. Speak to our Lord about them and ask for clarity and guidance. Keep track of what happens afterward.

† Take that same list of key influences and opportunities and discuss them with a trusted mentor or spiritual director, or even a wise friend. Listen to the other person's opinion and advice and include that in your own personal discernment.

† Take a long walk through a forest. Contemplate the many different species of plants and animals that grow and thrive there. Think about how the identity of each flows from within and how the very same soil, water, and sun bring out all those different identities. Pay attention to how that contemplation makes you feel.

Chapter 10: *Purpose*

The rush of new life at springtime isn't random. The cherry trees start to grow and blossom as they begin their mission of producing cherries. The apple trees launch out on the long process of producing their apples. Each plant reaches up and out to fulfill its purpose, and all their individual purposes harmonize to give spring its unconquerable, unquenchable beauty. This is the work of our loving Creator.

That same Creator gave us our purpose, too. We are created for happiness—everlasting happiness—and we find that happiness through living in communion with God.[3] Of course, that communion with God looks different for each of us. It involves a unique combination of experiences, relationships, and virtues that bring us into a deeper intimacy with God. And that's why each of us has to learn

---

[3] The most concise expression of our purpose comes from the *Catechism of the Catholic Church*: "Man is made to live in communion with God, in whom he finds happiness" (*CCC* 45). In the same vein, the catechism also quotes a well-known expression from St. Augustine, who had a knack for this kind of thing: "Our hearts are restless until they rest in God."

how to give a personalized name to our purpose.
Maybe the phrase "living in communion with God"
is enough for you; maybe it makes your heart ring
and galvanizes your desires and your energies. But
maybe it doesn't. In that case, find a phrase that
does.

Whatever the case, the search for purpose—for
truly knowing why we exist, where we come from,
and where we are going—is a fundamental human
need. We ignore that search at our own hazard.
Purpose is necessary for our existential health,
just as purpose is the melody at the heart of the
beautiful symphony of spring.

Maybe you have already found your calling
in life and are energetically engaged in living
it out. Maybe you are still seeking it. In either
case, the conviction that your life truly has a
purpose, a meaning, is a conviction that needs to
be frequently refreshed. Otherwise life becomes
either overwhelming or underwhelming; we get
lost in a tangle of exhausting overcommitment or
we drown in a suffocating sea of meaninglessness.
Without purpose, the bright vibrancy of spring
would fade to drab grayness. No flowers would
reach for the sky. No trees would stretch their
limbs. No birds would welcome the sunrise with
their joyous songs.

We are made to find our happiness by living
in communion with God. Yet each of us needs

to discover this for ourselves, existentially. Only then will our lives be able to blossom and take their proper place in the gorgeous and everlasting garden of eternity.

This primitive and unerasable need for purpose opened up a new world for me when I was in college, in a surprising way. It's rare to have a vivid memory of your first encounter with someone who later became a close friend. It's even rarer for a first encounter with a work of art to be memorable. Yet I can still remember my first experience of Donatello's life-size marble sculpture of St. George, an encounter that happened decades ago.

I was spending a college semester abroad in Florence, Italy. That day, we were visiting the Bargello, one of Florence's great sculpture museums. We made it to the second floor of the medieval palace and turned the corner into the Donatello room—a feast for any eyes, especially for those of a college kid studying art history. Almost immediately my attention was riveted by a marble figure on the far side of the cavernous space. It was as if that figure was addressing me personally, vehemently demanding my full attention.

Everything else faded into the background. I turned away from the group tour and stepped through the maze of other sculptures, drawn irresistibly until I found myself face to face with St George.

As in all of Donatello's sculptures, the stone was so perfectly molded that the skin looked as if it would be soft to the touch, and the marble seemed to vanish within the entrancing depiction of the various materials compromising the figure's clothing and accouterments—the sword, the armor, the cape. The proportions were effortlessly natural, and the entire composition seemed to be breathing.

I couldn't explain the poignant reaction I was having simply by observing Donatello's technical mastery. He had captured more, much more. That "more," whatever it was, pierced me, resonated in the depths of my soul, called out to the very core of my identity.

St. George, the ancient tradition goes, was a Cappadocian officer in the Roman Imperial Guard, raised by his mother in the Christian faith during the period of persecutions. While returning from a successful military campaign in Anatolia (modern-day Turkey), he rescued a local king's daughter from the clutches of some kind of terrible dragon, showing supernatural strength (which he attributed to his faith, not to himself) in defeating the monster. Later, he professed his faith boldly before the Emperor Diocletian, who used blandishment and torture to try and make him recant (it was illegal to be Christian at the time, since Christians refused to worship the false pagan gods of the Roman Empire), but all to no avail. The saint continued to profess his faith, convert witnesses, and even perform miracles as the persecuting authorities attempted to break his spirit. He finally received the martyr's crown by being beheaded in the first years of the fourth century.

Donatello's *St. George* is imbued with what every human heart yearns for and needs, and for what I was passionately searching as a young man: this mesmerizing marble figure embodies passionate and life-giving purpose. This man, standing with this weight slightly forward, his head held high, and his gaze intent on the horizon before him, knows what his life is for. He knows where he is going: to use all his strength to defend what is true and noble against the vicious attacks of evil. And that destination is filling him with elegant determination, with unwavering meaning, and also with a dynamic joy that brings an almost otherworldly light to his marble features.

Yes, St. George was a soldier, and he remains a patron saint of soldiers. But he was first and foremost a soldier of Jesus Christ, eager to bear witness to his Lord and further Jesus' kingdom of justice and love on earth, to the point of risking his reputation, his career, his fortune, and even his life. This purpose united and elevated his natural gifts and talents to the point that he became a saint.

This is the power that God wants to give to us,

that power that comes from having a true purpose, worthy of the inestimable dignity of every human heart and capable of unifying all the pieces of life that a modern world has left painfully fragmented.

That sculpture somehow gave me a taste of that transforming power of purpose, and I began to desire a fuller share of it. The desire was so intense that I still consider that encounter as the first one on my path to the priesthood. It was the first inkling of my vocation, the first sound of my personal calling.

If you were commissioned by the local Armorer's Guild to fashion a life-sized figure of such a saint, as Donatello was in 1415, where would you start? Most artists choose the dramatic encounter with the dragon. But Donatello didn't. He chose simply to show the man himself. And that choice made all the difference—at least to me.

Donatello's St. George stands straight and tall in his armor and cloak, bareheaded, leaning slightly on his shield, the tip of which is touching the ground in front of him. His strength, his youth, his vigor all shine forth brilliantly. But something else, some mysterious characteristic, brings them all together and elevates them. That elusive quality—enhanced by the technical perfection and reverential human beauty of the figure—was what struck such a deep chord in my own heart when I first encountered the sculpture.

It took years of reflection and admiration before I was able to put a word to that mysterious quality. But I think now I know what it is.

Making It Your Own

† Choose one sentence from this chapter that really resonated in your heart or compose a one-sentence summary. Write it on a sticky note. Put it where you will see it during the week as a reminder that your life has purpose.

† Take time to write down your understanding of the meaning of life. Try to find a way to express it that inspires and energizes you.

† Get together with two or three good friends and ask them to do the same thing—to write down their own personal description of the meaning of life. Read your descriptions to each other. Try to pick out the similarities and differences and discover what they mean for each one of you.

† Make a list of all your major commitments. Then describe how each one fits in with the purpose of your life. How would you live them differently if you were habitually more aware of their deeper meaning?

† If you're unsure of the meaning of your life, commit to search out a deeper understanding of it. As a first step, meet with a mentor, a spiritual director, or a wise acquaintance and ask one of them how he or she found the meaning of his or her life.

† True meaning in life comes from loving God and loving our neighbor. These are the two great commandments that Jesus taught us. But this fallen world often tries to substitute other false meanings for that true one. The most common substitutes are popularity, pleasure, power, and money (sometimes identified with professional success). Which of those do you feel tempted to embrace as a shortcut to meaning? How will you resist that temptation this week?

Chapter 11: *Beauty*

Beauty is that which gives pleasure upon being seen, according to perhaps the greatest philosopher and theologian of Western civilization, St. Thomas Aquinas. A more modern saint, Pope John Paul II, described beauty as God's goodness made visible. Without a doubt, both of these definitions apply to the beauty particular to springtime.

Our hearts beat faster when we drive along a majestic row of blossoming cherry trees. Our eyes widen at the jubilant blooms of dogwoods and crabapple trees. We don't want to look away when we spot a field bursting with wildflowers or the edge of a forest where the trees are just beginning to display their leaves. These sights—not to mention spring's delicious aromas and luxurious breezes—fill us with delight and a pure, refreshing pleasure. Springtime is certainly not shy about showing off its beauty.

And then it's over. The blossoms fall, the intense colors fade, the exultation settles down, and summer begins. And although summer has breathtaking beauties, those of springtime pass away.

That's how it is with all earthly beauty. It passes. Or we become accustomed to it and it no longer moves us as dramatically as it did at first. And this is good. This is natural. We are not meant to live in the intensity of spring all the time. Spring blossoms are meant to open a tree up to be fertilized and fruitful. The blossoms lead to the fruit, but if the blossoms don't fade and fall away, the fruit will never come.

This is a lesson we have forgotten. We have come to desire perpetual youth, perpetual springtime beauty. Our consumer society is bursting with products guaranteed to make fifty-year-old women look like they are twenty-five and sixty-year-old men have the muscle tone of teenagers. Why would a healthy fifty-year-old woman want to look like she were twenty-five? Why would a healthy sixty-year-old man want to look like a teenager? Why do we habitually disregard the value of our elders? Older and wiser cultures have always looked up to their elders with appreciation, esteem, and docility.

I was given a powerful lesson in this regard during the months before I joined the seminary. When I first told a priest that I felt a call to the priesthood I was a new Catholic, and he advised me to wait. He thought I should give it some time so I didn't confuse my call to become Catholic with a call to become a priest. So I followed his advice and continued with my normal life.

Soon afterward I met a wonderful young woman, and we hit it off immediately. We started to date. I did tell her that I was discerning a call to the priesthood, but it didn't keep us from developing a beautiful friendship and taking the first steps of courtship.

As we grew closer, I began to realize that I truly loved this woman. I also saw that we were a good match. Given our life situations and the way the relationship was progressing, I recognized that the next step was to move toward engagement. It wouldn't be fair to either one of us to simply draw things out, as if our dating was merely some kind of entertainment to fill our time. As you can imagine, this became a frequent topic in my prayer and personal reflection.

Searching my heart, I discovered something that surprised me. My love for this woman was deep and sincere—more than anything I had experienced before. At the same time, I heard the Lord calling me into the priesthood with greater clarity. Being honest with myself, I couldn't doubt it. At first this confused me. Why would God give me such a pure and real love for this woman if he were calling me to be his priest and to serve his Church in lifelong celibacy?

One afternoon while I was praying the rosary on the shores of Lake Michigan, I saw what was happening. It was precisely because I truly loved this woman that I couldn't marry her. She deserved a husband who could give his whole heart to her, a true and authentic husband in the fullest sense of the word. I was passionately convinced of that, because I cared for her deeply. And I, though I loved her, could never be that for her, because the deepest core of my being, the heart of my heart, was already dedicated to God alone—he had called me and I wanted to say yes to that call.

The beauty of this woman didn't belong to me. She wasn't some *thing* that I could claim and consume and possess. Her personal beauty—her inner beauty as well as her outer beauty—was a gift God had given to this world, and that gift needed to be respected and honored, not selfishly devoured. The right way for me to respect and honor her was to release her—God was calling me to marry his Church, and so he clearly had other and better plans for her than marrying me.

Now I can clearly see how that process of discovery played itself out. But while I was in the midst of it, I struggled and suffered—we both did. And yet, through that experience God began to teach me to appreciate and be inspired by his many beautiful gifts—especially the beauty of *persons*—without having to possess them.

The only explanation for our current bias toward physical beauty is that we have lost touch with the wisdom of the seasons. We have become obsessed with the explosive beauty of spring to such an extent that we no longer know how to appreciate the beauties of summer, fall, and winter, which are just as real. We have forgotten that all earthly beauty is passing, and its purpose is to inspire us along our journey into eternity.

Perhaps this is most evident in the epidemic-like proliferation of pornography in our digital world. Staggering numbers of men and women are falling prey to the debilitating and insidious blandishments of this false reality. Addictions in this area are rampant, and even morally neutral sociological studies are showing that these addictions are shredding our social fabric. The sublime beauty of the human body and human sexuality is being falsified and commercialized to an astonishing degree. Somehow, millions of our fellow human beings have come to prefer artificial flowers to the real thing simply because the plastic blossoms never fade. The fact that they are an illusion, a cold and lifeless imitation of true and fruitful beauty, is simply ignored.

That's not the only sign of our being out of touch with the wisdom of the seasons. It also shows up in our compulsion for recording even our smallest experiences with a digital photo and a digital share. We can become so obsessed with capturing all our experiences and freezing them into our social media profile that we actually lose the capacity to enjoy them as profoundly as we are called to.

How can we regain the wisdom of the seasons? How can we relearn to love the beauty of springtime without idolizing it and blinding ourselves to the beauty of the other seasons? It may be as simple as opening our eyes and shutting off our phones.

The same God who poured his goodness into springtime has also poured his goodness into summer and autumn and winter. The same God who created us with the ability to appreciate the glamorous beauty of movie stars has also given us the ability to appreciate his goodness as it shows itself in every person of any age. If we want to see it, we can. If we look for it, we will find it: "Search, and you will find…for the one who searches always finds" (Matthew 7:7–8, the *Jerusalem Bible*).

If we can just remember that all material beauty is *meant* to fade, that it is just an inkling of the enduring beauty of spiritual maturity and the everlasting beauty of God, then we will be able to delight in all the goodness and beauty of this world without gripping any of it too tightly. We will be able to enjoy it, to respect it, and to honor it, instead of compulsively consuming, possessing, and obliterating it. This will free us from our blindness.

God teaches us his lessons personally, not generically. And I certainly don't believe that everyone has to fall in love while discerning a call to the priesthood to rediscover the beauty of the seasons. But spiritual freedom is something he wants for each of us. And that comes from learning to appreciate the beauty in all of God's gifts, while at the same time respecting their transience and hearing their true message.

Let's glory in the beauties of spring while they last. Then release them when they pass, trusting that other beauties are yet to come. Let's honor them by respecting and remembering them, not by fearfully turning them into sterile plastic mockeries of truly vital blossoms.

Making It Your Own

† Choose one sentence from this chapter that really resonated in your heart or compose a one-sentence summary. Write it on a sticky note. Put it where you will see it throughout the week as a reminder to rejoice in the beauties of spring without being compulsive about them.

† It's easy to lose the beauty of a precious moment because we desperately want to capture it in a picture or share it on a post. This week, dedicate one full day to simply enjoying moments without trying to preserve them, except in your own memory.

† What are you afraid of losing? Things, relationships, status, reputation? Take time to write in a journal your biggest fears. Then prayerfully apply the wisdom of the seasons to all of them. Which ones do you need to release in order to be free to enjoy them as God wants you to?

† What role does multitasking play in your life? Most recent studies tend to agree that

multitasking isn't good for our emotional or physical health. It's better for us to fully focus on one thing at a time and calmly but diligently dedicate ourselves to it. This is linked to the wisdom of the seasons. Spring doesn't try to be summer, too. What can you do this week to bring greater calm and focus to your life?

† What do you tend to compulsively consume? Take a step back from that and reflect on it. What is its true purpose in the world and how can you release it to make that purpose be fulfilled in your own life? If you aren't sure, take time this week to get together with a wise friend or mentor to talk about some of your compulsive tendencies or fears.

† If it is true, as Pope St. John Paul II wrote, that beauty is God's goodness made visible, then all the beautiful things of life are actually reflections of God. Take time this week to think deeply about the most beautiful things you have ever seen or experienced. Ask the Lord to show you how they are connected to him. Prayerfully seek to find his face in those reflections of his goodness and allow that to deepen your love for him, as well as your awareness of his love for you.

Chapter 12: *Faith*

Do you remember how you reacted to the first signs of spring when you were a child? Or maybe you have young children of your own and you can just look at their reactions and see them happening in real time.

The first signs of spring stir up energy in children's hearts. Their eyes light up when the snow starts to melt. They want to go outside without a coat on. They want to play in the sun and leave the musty basement behind. It doesn't take much to stimulate that eagerness. Just a warm day with icicles dripping themselves away. Just a little shoot of something green peeking up through the mud and the slush. Just a small sign of spring, even a tiny little *sign* of a sign—that's all a child's heart needs to alight the faith and give it new life.

Personally, I think this is part of what Jesus had in mind when he told his followers, "Amen, I say to you, unless you turn and become like children, you will not enter the kingdom of heaven," (Matthew 18:3). Children are still open to new possibilities. In fact, their whole worldview is all about new possibilities. They are just discovering reality, and so it's not strange for them to expect that reality has surprises in store, that clues to greater things are all around them. Faith comes naturally to them.

And then we grow up. We experience disappointments. Sometimes very painful disappointments. People let us down. Things go wrong. Reality takes on a harsh aspect and we feel a need to protect ourselves from future possibilities instead of running forth enthusiastically to meet them. We become hesitant, fearful, maybe even cynical. We are habitually suspicious instead of easily encouraged, looking for the trick and the trap behind every promise instead of the treasure. The snow starts to melt, and our eyes darken instead of lighting up. It's going to get warm and then freeze up again and the roads will be treacherous. Green buds form on the trees and we shake our heads because it's just too early. Spring is going to be blighted by a late frost, we just know it.

Which is a better way to live life, like the child who needs barely a nudge to believe in spring, or like the jaded pessimist who only believes when belief is no longer necessary?

We often ask people if they believe in God. And when we meet someone with weak faith, we find ourselves wanting to help strengthen it. When we meet someone with strong, robust faith, we want to tap into it to bolster our own. In a sense, we recognize that even if we have faith, we want a more vibrant faith. We are like the man in the Gospels who came to Jesus and asked him to heal his son. He said to the Lord, "If you can do anything, have compassion on us and help us!" And Jesus gave him a surprising reply: "'If you can!' Everything is possible to one who has faith." Then it was the man's turn to surprise Jesus. The boy's father cried out, "I do believe, help my unbelief!" (from Mark 9:14–29).

I just love that prayer. That's how I feel, on a daily basis. Yes, I believe in God's loving, wise, and all-powerful providence. Yet I still have to resist temptations to worry and stress. Yes I believe that God will never abandon us—and yet he permits so much suffering in the world! "I believe, Lord, but help my unbelief! Strengthen my faith!"

Another one of my favorite lines from the Bible is the one spoken to Jesus by the blind man to whom Jesus said, "What do you want me to do for you?" The blind man replied to him, "Master, I want to see" (Mark 10:51). I, too, want to see! I want to be able to see the hand of God in all things, at all times. I want to be able to see how I should act in every situation, what I should say, what I should avoid, how God wants me to serve and what he wants me to do. *Master, I do believe, and I want to see! Increase my faith and open my eyes!*

❦

Many beautiful religious memorials take place in the springtime. Easter, of course, is the best one. But one of the lesser-known celebrations is worth a bit of reflection, too.

Every March 25 for the past 1,500 years or so, Catholic Christians throughout the world have celebrated the Solemnity of the Annunciation. This commemorates the scene from the Gospels where the Archangel Gabriel appeared to the Blessed Virgin Mary and announced that she had been chosen to the be the Virgin Mother of Jesus, the promised Savior of the world. Christians have always cherished Mary's response to that announcement as the quintessential expression of deep, simple, childlike faith, the kind of faith that unleashes the saving power of God's grace in this crazy world. It required her to change her plans, as you can imagine, but she accepted that and then said to Gabriel: "Behold, I am the handmaid of the Lord. May it be done to me according to your word" (Luke 1:38).

Mary's response shows that she *believed* the angel's promise even though she was only a teenager, even though she was poor, even though she had (probably) never had any angelic visions before (she had no recorded visions afterward, either). God's word and the true resonance it produced in her heart were enough. She didn't doubt or resist: *she believed.* She let her heart sing at the first sign of spring.

Whenever I pray about the annunciation, the first thing that comes to mind is another sculpture by Donatello. Like his sculpture of St. George, it is in the Italian city of Florence, was created in the 1400s, and you can still see it today. Funnily enough, in medieval and renaissance times, Florence followed its own yearly calendar, and New Year's Day was March 25—the Solemnity of the Annunciation, the beginning of spring.

We are used to seeing this type of depiction of the annunciation, with the angel bowing and giving his message to Mary. But Donatello was the first sculptor to depict this scene with such palpable drama. And it was the drama that struck a chord with me.

On the one hand, we can see that St. Gabriel is interrupting our Lady. She is just closing her little prayer book with one hand, and with the other hand she is pulling her cloak over her as if to protect herself. Her right knee is turning away from the angel, while her left foot is still planted and hasn't yet caught up with her body's motion. But even as her body is moving away from the angel, as if she is surprised or frightened, her face and head show that she is mesmerized by the vision and the angelic presence.

Isn't that how it is with all of us? When God breaks into our lives—interrupting our routine with an invitation to repent or to serve in a new way, or to somehow follow him more closely—isn't our automatic reaction one of fright or resistance? We say, "Well, Lord, I have a lot to do, and I don't think your idea is going to fit into my plans." And yet, even as we resist, there is a place in our hearts, at the very core of our being, where we feel the excitement and the draw of the adventure. At that level, the level of our childlike faith, we still know that we are made for God and that accepting his invitation is the sure path to the meaningful, worthwhile life that we truly desire. Our true self wants to pay attention to God's voice and believe, but our brokenness and skepticism and selfish tendencies tend to spur us to flee from the Lord. This truly is the drama of faith: *I believe, help my unbelief!*

In Mary's case, the interior battle of the drama of faith was much less violent than in our case. She was preserved from original sin and free from personal sin. And so, though the angel's message caused her to be "greatly troubled" (Luke 1:29), she recovered quickly.

May is the spring month *par excellence.* And in the ancient tradition of our faith, May is celebrated as Mary's month. This spring, let's permit the signs of new life to rejuvenate our faith, and, like Mary, start out afresh on the adventure of grace to which God never ceases inviting us.

Making It Your Own

† Choose one sentence from this chapter that really resonated in your heart or compose a one-sentence summary. Write it on a sticky note. Put it where you will see it throughout the week as a reminder that we are called to "walk by faith, not by sight" (2 Corinthians 5:7).

† What life areas look more cynical than childlike? What can you do this week to curb your cynicism and refresh your childlike faith?

† Think about your most treasured and beautiful childhood memories. Write them down, describing them in detail to relive those experiences. Then reflect on *why* they are so beautiful to you. What aspects of yourself do you like when you see yourself in that experience? What has happened to those aspects over the years? What can you do to recover or revitalize some of the more basic, healthy, and pure elements of your own personality?

† Prayerfully reflect on some of the harsh experiences you have had to go through in life. Do it *prayerfully* so that you don't feel alone, but in the presence of God as you remember them. Ask God to show you how they may have damaged or bolstered your faith. Ask him to show you how to integrate those experiences

into a new springtime for your faith in him. Write your response in a letter to God.

† Take time this week to read over the whole biblical passage of the annunciation. It's in Luke 1:26–38. Read it slowly, picturing how it unfolded and what the Blessed Virgin must have been feeling. Then speak to God about the feelings that surge up in your own heart.

† Go with a few close friends or family members on an old-fashioned picnic. Make sure everything fits into the "old-fashioned-picnic" category. Give yourself plenty of time. Then give yourself permission to enjoy it thoroughly, as children do. Later, spend time prayerfully reflecting on that experience. What is God trying to tell you through it?

The author, Fr. John Bartunek, LC, STD, splits his time between Michigan, where he continues his writing apostolate and assists at Our Lady Queen of the Family Retreat Center in Oxford, and Rome, where he teaches theology at the Pontifical Athenaeum Regina Apostolorum. He is the author of several books, including *The Better Part* and *Inside the Passion: An Insider's Look at the Passion of the Christ.* Fr. Bartunek became a member of the Catholic Church in 1991, was ordained a Catholic priest in 2003, and earned his doctorate in moral theology in 2010. His online retreats are available at RCSpirituality.org, and he answers questions about the spiritual life at SpiritualDirection.com.

CPSIA information can be obtained
at www.ICGtesting.com
Printed in the USA
FFOW05n2036220116